He Loves Me NOT . . . He Loves Me

by

Sandra Nunn

and

Rose McCormick Brandon

Copyright © 2012 by Sandra Nunn and Rose McCormick Brandon

He Loves Me Not . . . He Loves Me
by Sandra Nunn and Rose McCormick Brandon

Printed in the United States of America

ISBN 9781624196041

All rights reserved solely by the author. The author guarantees all contents are original and do not infringe upon the legal rights of any other person or work. No part of this book may be reproduced in any form without the permission of the author. The views expressed in this book are not necessarily those of the publisher.

Unless otherwise indicated, Bible quotations are taken from the New International Version. Copyright © 1984 by The Zondervan Corporation.

For more information:
Sandra Nunn
ernestsandranunn@yahoo.ca

www.xulonpress.com

Dedicated to my beloved, Ernie

ACKNOWLEDGEMENTS

Several people read the manuscript. Each one suggested changes that contributed to the finished product. Thank you to Patricia Capy, Anne Laidlaw, Mary Lucchetti and Tamara Svantesson. Special thanks to Heather Collins for her meticulous edit.

Thanks to Ernie Nunn for checking the book through several re-writes, for his wholehearted support of the project and his willingness to share how God transformed his life. Ernie's story makes Sandra's story possible.

Rose McCormick Brandon
and
Sandra Nunn

CONTENTS

Foreword v
Introduction xiii
Chapter 1 My Christmas Miracle 17
Chapter 2 Child of Adversity 22
Chapter 3 Immigrant Life 29
Chapter 4 Meeting Jesus 37
Chapter 5 Romance and Marriage 43
Chapter 6 The Explosion 56
Chapter 7 Life in my Dysfunctional Home 63
Chapter 8 My Search for Significance 72
Chapter 9 Queen of Clean and Clutter Control 74
Chapter 10 Adjusting to my new Husband 78
Chapter 11 Crossing the Street 82
Chapter 12 Our Mission 85
Chapter 13 Changes 93
Chapter 14 My Continuing Love Story 99
A Final Word 105

FOREWORD

He loves me not...He loves me - what an apt description of the life journey of my friend, Sandra Nunn. I first met Sandra and her husband, Ernie, in 1977 when I became their pastor in Simcoe, Ontario. It didn't take long for me to learn that behind Sandra's jovial nature lurked a private world of marital disappointment and ongoing conflict. How wonderful for me, many years later, to become aware of God's miracle working power in the lives of this couple who were content to keep living in quiet desperation.

When Ernie and Sandra came to Winnipeg to share their story, soon after the transformation of their marriage, I was totally taken by the genuine expression of love between them.

I saw their love, I heard it, and now you get the opportunity to read about it. Here's a couple who had given up on ever experiencing the joy and love that God wanted for them. You will thrill when you read how God replaced their pain, hurt and regrets with love. You'll see how He used His creative power to bring about Godly sorrow and true repentance which led to forgiveness and love.

Sandra's story assures us again that, with God, there are no impossible situations.

I knew Sandra and Ernie before their transformation and I know them now. Trust me; this is a redemptive miracle of God's amazing grace.

Pastor Bruce Martin
Calvary Temple, Winnipeg, Manitoba

INTRODUCTION

*L*ate 2011, I was knee-deep in a project and determined to finish it. I'd been writing a novel off and on for years and decided that 2012 would be my year to complete it. That meant keeping focused, putting aside smaller projects, and guarding my time.

Then the phone rang.

"I've been reading your articles for a long time and you're the one I want to write my book."

Flattering words for a writer to hear. But, bad timing. I knew the amount of work involved in writing someone else's story. Also, I didn't want to mix the fiction side of my brain with the non-fiction side. I planned to immerse myself in the dreamy world of fictional characters, find the rhythm of their heart beats and listen to the timbre of their voices.

But, I didn't say no. I explained to the caller my goal of finishing the novel. I ended our conversation by saying, "Write out the main points of your story and call me back mid-January." If the caller wasn't serious, she wouldn't write anything and that would be the end of that. I sensed the caller's upbeat personality through the phone lines, a woman of passion. If she is serious, I thought, it would be nice to meet her.

Mid-January, the woman with the story called again. She'd written several pages and wondered if we could get together and talk about doing a book. No harm in meeting, I thought.

Sandra Nunn entered my living room on a cold Tuesday afternoon in January 2012. "What's your story about?" I asked.

"It's a love story," she said. Those words got Sandra started. For the next three hours, while Sandra talked, I tapped fragments of her story onto my laptop. By late afternoon, I liked Sandra, and I detected God's fingerprint on her story.

When I heard God's eternal story humming inside Sandra's story, I wanted to write it, for Him. People need to hear and see God at work in the lives of ordinary people.

At the end of our first session, we made plans to meet again, and again. This book is the result of many hours of conversation between Sandra and me in my living room. I asked questions. She answered in her candid way, telling stories, reliving her memories.

At times, I got lost in Sandra's story, sitting for hours pouring words into the document that became this book. My novel took a back seat to Sandra's love story . . . for a while.

Introduction

There's nothing hidden about Sandra. She has a strong streak of humor and a warm heart. And no trace of guile. People easily connect with her. Everyone who reads her story will benefit from it.

This is Sandra's story. Read it and share it.

For His Honour,
Rose McCormick Brandon
rosembrandon@yahoo.ca

Chapter 1

My Christmas Miracle

On Christmas Day 2003, I fell in love with my husband again. My husband, Ernie, and I attended a family celebration at my parents' home. Dinner had been served, gifts opened, and mountains of wrapping paper and clutter cleared away. The kids retreated downstairs and the adults dispersed to different parts of the house in search of a place to relax. I sank into a comfortable chair in the living room, exhausted from doing dishes and tidying the kitchen. My sister Janie, and her husband, Dennis, sat on a sofa on the opposite side of the room. Ernie stood beside them; they were chatting. Grateful for a quiet moment, I leaned back in my chair, inattentive to their conversation.

Then these words drifted across the room. Ernie said, "I really would like to be nice to my wife and treat her as a loved woman."

My jaw dropped. Did I really hear those words from my husband of almost forty years? We'd lived separately, but under the same roof, for over three decades. When I looked over at him, I saw Ernie wipe away tears. Those three, Janie, Dennis and Ernie, continued their conversation but I didn't hear anything else they said.

I didn't go to Ernie or make any comment. A bit bewildered, I sat quietly and contemplated the meaning of Ernie's strange admission. *He wants to love me again*, I thought. We once loved one another, but that young love had vanished.

Evening came and our family gathering began to break up. Ernie and I loaded our things into the car and headed home. Without uttering a word, he reached across the seat, clasped my hand in his and held it as he drove. I couldn't remember the last time our fingers had touched. I didn't ask him about the tidbit of conversation I'd overheard.

As we cruised through the night, our car became a sanctuary of healing. In the silence, God worked a miracle of reconciliation between us. Each kilometer we traveled took us farther from the anger that had driven us apart. The sensation was pure awe. I like to talk and my mind was full of questions but I didn't want to break the spell of happiness that enveloped us. For a half-hour, we floated down the highway caught up in the greatest miracle either of us had experienced.

When we arrived home, Ernie got out of the car, hurried to my side and opened the door for me. Another thing that hadn't happened in decades. As he parked the car and unloaded our things, I went

My Christmas Miracle

into the kitchen. I was standing at the counter when Ernie came up behind me and caressed my face and hugged me.

At that moment, I began to suspect he might be playing games, making me think there was a chance for us when in reality, hope for our fractured marriage had vanished long ago. I wanted to believe in him but Ernie's cruel remarks had hurt me too often. He hadn't touched me with affection since our mid-twenties. His remark earlier in the day about wanting to love me, holding my hand on the drive home and now his physical closeness in the kitchen, all of it became too much for me. I wanted to scream at him to get away.

Instead, I asked, "Why the change?"

That's when Ernie told me what had happened to him six months earlier.

While asleep, Ernie heard someone call his name. He awoke and looked at the clock - one-thirty in the morning. He went to my room, opened the door and said, "Sandra, what do you want?"

I was sound asleep. Ernie went back to his room and sat on the edge of the bed. A scripture came to his mind: "They (the disciples) left everything and followed Him." (Luke 5:11). Was God speaking to him, Ernie wondered.

In the stillness, Ernie whispered a response. "I don't have anything of value to walk away from."

It wasn't money, a business, or any other tangible thing that God wanted Ernie to give up. Again, the voice spoke. "Leave your bitterness, anger and unforgiveness." Ernie had lived in spiritual darkness for a long time. This personal message from God rekindled his faith.

In our kitchen that night, months after Ernie's God encounter, tears glistened in his eyes as he told me the story. His middle-of-the-night drama humbled him. I saw genuine sorrow in his face, sorrow for his years of anger toward God, toward me, and toward the people in our church that hurt him. The answer to my question, "Why the change?" was that God, for the previous six months, had been transforming Ernie. Loving me again was part of that transformation.

On that life-changing night, after the Lord told Ernie to lay down bitterness, anger and unforgiveness, he knelt by his bed and prayed. With many tears, he confessed his sins and re-committed his life to Jesus Christ.

Until that Christmas Day in 2003, Ernie kept this life-changing experience to himself, afraid people might think him mentally unstable. God calling his name seemed like a preposterous story.

Ernie kept silent about his experience for another reason. He wanted his changed behavior to speak for itself. In retrospect, I had noticed something different about Ernie during those six months. A contented peacefulness perhaps? Whatever it was, I ignored it. His behaviour wearied me. I no longer hoped for good things from him. It took years for me to accept our estranged relationship. When I did accept it, he became like an unwanted houseguest to me. I begged him, and then ordered him to leave our home. He refused. Stubbornly, I also refused to leave.

My Christmas Miracle

Earlier in our marriage, when hope still existed, I fantasized about a return to our young love, the love we had as teenagers and newlyweds, but my dreams died. After years of living with an angry man, I resigned myself to an unloving marriage.

On that Christmas Day in 2003 I wasn't prepared for a miracle. It came as a surprise. At first, I was afraid to believe in it but Ernie patiently proved that the change in him is genuine. Every day since that momentous drive home he has treated me with more love than I thought possible. Today, we have a marriage far above anything I envisioned for us, something beyond my young bride dreams of a happy-ever-after life.

The best Christmas present I've received in my whole life is a husband who loves me. I waited a long time for the gift. When it came, it came with more kindness, more gentleness, and more romance than I believed possible.

Ernie and I have dubbed this present phase of our relationship *our second chance to dance.*

Chapter 2

Child of Adversity

I'm often asked why I stayed in an unloving marriage for decades. Was I waiting for a miracle? Partly. Did I feel duty-bound to stay? Sometimes. But the best answer lies in the circumstances of my early life. People who face hardships at a young age often develop steely courage and I believe this happened to me. I grew an indomitable spirit, and to a large extent, I also inherited this trait from my parents. Both were children of adversity.

In the 1930s, the German government forcibly removed thousands of children, most of them teenagers, from Poland and the Ukraine. They transported these young people into Germany and put them to work on farms. Many never saw their parents or siblings again. My father, Walter Senko, grew up in a Ukrainian family of sixteen children. Raised by grandparents, he lived in a household so poor the children bound rags on their feet in winter to keep them from freezing. One day, without warning, authorities descended on the Senko household and separated Walter, then fourteen, from his family. He was herded into a group of teenagers and taken to Germany.

My mother, Martha Kuziw, was a sensitive child who adored her mother. She was taken from her family at age twelve. A few years later, while working on the same farm in Germany, Walter and Martha met and fell in love. As World War II progressed, Germany ordered every available man to join their army. Anyone who didn't support Hitler's effort to crush the Allied Forces was sent to prison. Walter Senko refused to fight for Germany. His Ukrainian brothers belonged to the Russian army and he didn't want to meet them in battle.

To avoid arrest, Walter hid in forests, sheds and barns. He depended on the kindness of German farmers for food and shelter. One night, a property owner reported to police that Walter was hiding in one of his out-buildings. In mid 1944, his days as a fugitive ended. Arrested and charged, Walter entered the dark world of Buchenwald Prison.

Martha, now pregnant, continued to work in the fields. She heard of Walter's arrest and believed she'd never see him again. Alone, amongst foreigners, and growing larger each day, Martha's losses caught up to her. Tears flowed unstoppable. A lump of despair settled in her chest. She cried for her parents and siblings. She cried for Walter and for the child growing within her.

Continual weeping drained Martha of emotional and physical strength. Her value as a farmhand was based on her ability to work but a broken spirit and bulging body made it impossible for her to keep up. Martha was committed to a hospital. There, in February 1945, Walter and Martha's baby girl entered the world. Shortly after birth, the baby, Oksana Senko, was taken from her mother and placed in an orphanage in another city.

That's how my life began - as Oksana Senko. Oksana means *"Praise God."*

With my parents separated by the tragic circumstances of World War II, and unable to care for me, I spent the first few months of my life in an orphanage. If the war had not ended later in the year of my birth, my life would have had a different outcome.

Rendered powerless by his imprisonment, Walter worried day and night for Martha and their baby. Would he die in Buchenwald, another insignificant casualty of the war? The only prayer Walter knew was one he learned in his grandparents' Greek Orthodox Church in the Ukraine – the Lord's Prayer. In prison, he repeated it many times each day.

One day an American reporter came to the prison and snapped a picture of a group of men standing wide-eyed and gaunt behind a barbed wire fence. Many years later, Life Magazine published this photo. It shows Walter, age 22, tall, his cheeks hollow, peering into the camera's lens, a hopeful glint in his eye. *Could the photographer's presence mean freedom was near? Would he soon see Martha and their baby?* Miserable months passed. Walter spent almost a year in Buchenwald. Then, miraculously, the war ended and his prison doors opened.

Released, Walter found many changes. Martha had disappeared. He didn't know where to begin his search for her or their baby. He decided to return to the place of his arrest, to the farmer who had turned him in to police. When the man saw the young Ukrainian on his property, he feared for his life. Walter told him he wasn't out for revenge, he needed help. "Just give me a bicycle and some food," he said. The farmer quickly bundled bread and cheese in a sack and wheeled a bicycle from his barn.

Walter set out on a six hundred kilometer journey to find Martha and their baby. Through many twists and turns, he discovered his wife had been sent to a mental hospital and his baby to an orphanage. First, he pedaled to the orphanage and convinced administrators he was the father of the Senko baby. They gave him one spare diaper and told him where to find Martha. Another long journey. Walter sold the bicycle and bought a train ticket. A young man unaccustomed to fatherhood, he boarded the train with me in one arm and the spare diaper tucked under the other.

Only a few months old, I don't remember the train trip but I'm certain as the wheels of that train clacked along, closer and closer to my mother, Walter Senko and I bonded as father and daughter. From the first day my head rested against his solid chest and I heard the beat of his heart, I loved him. Always resourceful, Dad rinsed one wet diaper at a time and held it out the window to dry. Release from prison renewed his hope for a better future. The joy and responsibility of fatherhood made him more determined than ever to make a good life for himself and his little family.

With me cradled in his arms, Dad arrived at the hospital to rescue my mother. She had suffered months of extreme anguish, believing her husband was likely dead and her child gone forever, possibly adopted by another family. Always a weepy woman, my mother's tears of sorrow turned into tears of gladness when she looked up from her hospital bed and saw her husband and her baby girl. That was Mom's day of liberation.

With all three Senkos freed and reunited, Walter and Martha found work on a farm that provided dormitory accommodations. During the day, they left me in a crib while they laboured in the fields. Each night, when they returned to our cubbyhole, they found me covered with bed bugs. They didn't complain about our living conditions or ask that my mother be allowed to stay with me during the day. Alive, together, with jobs and a roof over our heads, my parents felt grateful and enthusiastic about their future.

Besides farm work, Dad delivered for a bakery and juggled an assortment of other jobs. His devotion to hard work and determination kept the little Senko family fed and happy. In spite of separation from my parents in the first few months of my life, I quickly connected with them. Like three cords braided, my heart united with the hearts of Walter and Martha, a lovely condition that has lasted throughout my life.

Many desperate years, filled with trouble, confusion and displacement followed World War II. That difficult time required unusual sacrifice. Neither Walter nor Martha had parents, siblings or other relatives in Germany to support them. They fended for themselves.

In 1947, my parents applied for immigration to Canada. That year, the Canadian government passed its Citizenship Act, which made it easier for Europeans to immigrate. Any person sponsored by a Canadian citizen who promised to provide employment and housing could enter Canada. An aunt and uncle we'd never met became our Canadian sponsors. During the two years we waited for our papers, my brother Jerry was born. Dad told us how wonderful life would be when we arrived in Canada. I remember him saying we would have lots of food, including all the kielbasa we could eat.

In 1949, more than fifty thousand newcomers landed at Pier 21 in Halifax, Nova Scotia. Our excited family of four was among them. Everything we owned fit into a small suitcase. We had no family photographs, and no cherished trinkets. All these had been destroyed in the war. We landed in Canada unencumbered, ready to start a new life. For me, this meant not only a new country, but a new name – Sandra. I believe someone told my parents that this name was closest to the Ukrainian, Oksana. Sandra means *The Helper.*

Oksana, *Praise God.* Sandra, *The Helper.* The meanings of both names became like prophesies for my life.

Chapter 3

Immigrant Life

*F*rom Halifax, we traveled to Windham Centre, near Waterford, Ontario to the Kurzyna farm. There, a small, plain cottage, with a fresh coat of red paint, became our new home. Compared to our squalid accommodations in Germany, that neat cottage seemed like a mansion. We felt rich. And incredibly fortunate to live in Canada.

Like most farmers, Mom and Dad both worked long hours in the fields. At age four, I became principal babysitter for two year-old Jerry. Today, few parents would consider leaving a toddler in the care of a pre-schooler but in hard times people find unusual solutions to their problems. My parents didn't neglect us. To them, I wasn't a helpless little girl but a capable youngster. During the day while Mom worked in the fields, I made lunch for Jerry and me, mostly jam on bread, and played with him to keep him occupied. I was incredibly responsible for four, but my childish side still ruled.

He Loves Me Not . . . He Loves Me

What do two children left alone for hours each day do to amuse themselves? They get into trouble, of course. One day a cow strayed from the barn area and headed toward our house. The door was open and the cow took this as an invitation to enter. Jerry and I welcomed the animal's presence at first but when it struck us in the face with its swishing tail, we became frantic. The cow took advantage of our age and size. She clopped around the kitchen leaving dirty hoof marks and bits of manure, all the while licking food from the counter. I grabbed a wooden spoon and kept hitting her with it until she finally ambled back out the door. One short visit from that cow left our tidy kitchen in a complete mess. I tried to clean up, worried that my parents would be disappointed and angry. But when they returned from the fields and heard about our visit from the cow, they grinned with amusement.

On another occasion, bored by long hours alone, I sat Jerry in the corner next to a one hundred pound bag of flour my mother used for all our household baking. The bag was almost full. The thought occurred to me that dumping the flour onto Jerry's head would be an interesting past time. Cup after cup, I scooped the entire contents of the bag onto Jerry. Flour dust filled the air. Jerry sputtered and coughed. He almost suffocated. Thankfully, Jerry and I survived those early babysitting days. In spite of our poverty, and my childhood babysitting adventures, our family was a happy one.

As more children came along and my responsibilities grew, I begrudged looking after younger siblings. But I loved my mother and sought to please her. From an early age, I did my best to make her life easier. By six o'clock each evening, I had our house sparkling clean for her return from the fields. Then she could start dinner right away. Mom was a gentle spirit and always quick to show appreciation for my babysitting and cleaning. A few words of approval from her evaporated the complaints about heavy responsibilities that often simmered inside me.

Mom worked with my father in the fields her whole life. As we matured, Jerry and I took on other household duties. As the oldest girl and boy, it fell to us to milk the family cow every morning before going to school. I strained the milk into big jars and put them in the fridge. We made our own butter, sour cream and cottage cheese. They tasted much better than the product we buy in grocery stores today.

Besides working constantly, my poor mother was always pregnant. As younger children came along, they became my responsibility. I loved the babies after they arrived, but every time I found out about a pregnancy, I felt resentful about having one more kid to look after. Eventually, nine children blessed our household. After we immigrated to Canada, Patricia, Lilly, David, Walter, Steven, Ronnie and Janie were born.

I often missed school to help out at home. Mom and Dad explained to my teachers that they needed me to help plant and harvest the crops, and to look after the younger ones. But I didn't want anyone to need me. I wanted to stay in the classroom with my friends. Too many absences caused my grades to slip. I failed grades two and eleven. This humiliated me and blew a hole in my self-esteem.

Our family didn't know the meaning of the word vacation. We spent our summers in the field hoeing crops. All we knew was work. Labour in the home and in the fields, before and after school, and throughout the summer, filled my growing-up years. My parents passed their strong work ethic down to me. To this day, I can't figure out what people do on vacation. I can't imagine relaxing on a beach in the sun; I'm always working.

In the fields, I was the meticulous one, pulling each weed. It often took a whole day for me to finish one row. Jerry worked fast, doing double the work, but the next day, the weeds in his rows had already popped up again. My perfectionist tendencies showed early in life.

Mom taught me to do everything to the best of my ability. This too has remained with me. During my years at home, before marrying Ernie, I was our family's second mother. I helped get the younger siblings ready for school and put them on the bus that picked them up in front of our house. After that, I walked to school with the older ones, about a mile. Going to school was a day out for me. I looked forward to it. When classes ended, I came home to dirty dishes and more babysitting. After clean-up, I'd start the evening meal, a major accomplishment in a family as large as ours. I never enjoyed cooking but still strived to do it well. When Mom came in from the fields she would finish the meal. I began keeping a clean and orderly home to please my mother but, over time, it became a personal priority for me.

Saturday nights consisted of washing the children's socks, polishing their shoes and giving them a once-a-week bath. For years we used a portable galvanized tub, the same water for each person. (Dirty bath water must be the secret to beautiful skin because all my brothers and sisters are blessed with great skin.) Before putting them to bed, I laid out their church outfits for the next morning. While I looked after the children's needs, my mother spent Saturday evenings in the kitchen preparing food for the next day.

For the most part, my younger siblings accepted me as their second mother. But sometimes they'd run to my parents and accuse me of being bossy. I was bossy, of course, because if they got into trouble, it meant more work for me. One Sunday, I dressed all the children for church. When it was time to leave, I couldn't find David. After searching the grounds, I found him behind the barn swimming in a mud puddle with his church clothes on. We didn't have time to go to the beach so I guess this was his way of getting a swim. It's funny when I think of it now, but then I couldn't see the funny side of their antics. I was serious about making my younger siblings obey me.

On Sunday mornings we piled into one car, sitting on each other's laps. Like many families, we fought and argued all the way to church. After morning services, my parents opened the doors of our full house to many guests. No one had the courage to reciprocate. I complained to my mother about the unfairness of this but she didn't share my view. She explained that no one could accommodate a guest family of eleven and that mine was an unreasonable expectation. Individually, we visited our friends' homes. I cherished every invitation. Someone to serve and clean up after me in a quieter atmosphere – that was a treat for me.

In spite of my complaints, Mom and Dad opened the doors of our home to a steady stream of visitors. Everyone, especially children, wanted to come to the Senko home. My parents didn't worry about damage to their furniture or spots on the carpet. They focused on building relationships. In the relaxed, fun atmosphere of the Senko home, guests received lots of good food and encouraging words. Each one was made to feel special. We expected drop-in visitors and always welcomed them. Sadly, today we need a week's notice before guests arrive, and then, we still panic because our homes aren't perfect.

My parents extended hospitality to everyone. They never complained about guests, even when I surprised them by inviting all my classmates to our home after school. In my on-going effort to impress everyone I knew, I sometimes got carried away. In lieu of producing a pet pony, I once led a cow onto the front lawn and hopped onto her back while my classmates watched. Another time, I danced around our living room to convince them I was a tap-dancer. They seemed amazed at my talent. Mission accomplished. I never ran out of creative ways to make myself seem important. Once, when I arrived home with my unexpected guests, Dad left his work in the fields and went to the store to buy cake and food for the kids. Everyone who entered the Senko home received acceptance and kindness. No matter how many friends I invited to our busy home I was never reprimanded for it.

Our family quickly outgrew the farm cottage and Dad found a small twenty-five acre property with a two-bedroom house on it. This home too became a popular gathering place. Our house wasn't filled with fine furniture but my parents knew how to create an atmosphere of warmth and joy that drew people into our home.

I developed a close and loving relationship with my parents, but not an openly affectionate one. My self-worth came from work. My father says I never said no when asked to do anything. My love for both my parents is strong and their praise means a lot to me but, as a child, I felt awkward about kisses and hugs. I remember my youngest siblings sitting on Dad's knee but I have no memories of him snuggling with me. At six, some of them still bounced on his lap. By that age, I cleaned, cooked and babysat two children.

My childhood memories are filled with work. I don't hold a grudge about this. As the oldest child in the family, that's just the way life was for me. I was then, and still am, Sandra, *The Helper*. In Mom's later years, I cleaned her house every week. I did it out of love and because she showed so much appreciation. She too became responsible at a young age and slaved at physically demanding work her whole life. Easing her load always made me feel good.

When visitors came to our house, Mom would often tell them, "I don't know what I would do without my Oksana."

Those words thrilled me.

Chapter 4

Meeting Jesus

Shortly after our arrival in Canada, distant relatives living in Brantford, Ontario came to visit us in Waterford. We called them Auntie and Uncle Cebrowski. This couple told my parents about Jesus and they both accepted Him as Saviour. That event changed life for everyone in the Senko household. We started attending the Slavic Pentecostal Church in Waterford, an assembly made up of immigrants. That church became our second home. We attended morning and evening services on Sundays and Bible study every Wednesday night. Peter Gubic, a bachelor from Czechoslovakia, was our pastor. A refined gentleman, he spoke English well. I remember him most for treating me like an important person.

Our church was a stone building with an impressive set of steps that spanned the entire width of the structure. I found it fascinating and a little bit spooky. The man who built the church designed it according to a dream he had. He installed seven fire places on the upper floor. The building often doubled as a temporary home for immigrant families. It was in that strange and amazing place that I came to know Jesus.

As a little girl, I adored the Saviour. After each Sunday evening service, it was customary for the whole congregation to kneel around the front of the sanctuary. Together, we sent up prayers to Heaven. People wept without shame. We overheard one another's prayers and carried the weight of each other's burdens. I spent many hours at the altar in that church surrounded by children and adults. Jesus became as real to me as any member of my family, and my best Friend.

Our church leaders often read from the New Testament book of Acts and preached that everything the believers experienced in the first century could happen in our lives, including the ability to pray in languages we hadn't learned. When I was about six, while I was praying, the Holy Spirit gave me the ability to pray in a heavenly language. I've continued this practice throughout my life. Many times, praying in tongues saved me from wallowing in discouragement and hopelessness. Often, throughout my troubled marriage, I couldn't find words to express my need to God. In those times, I found release by praying in the Spirit.

Our church had a piano but no one to play it. Never one to turn down an opportunity for attention, when the pastor suggested I take on the role of pianist, I agreed. The congregation cooperated by singing slowly as a diligent eight year-old pounded notes with one finger. To my knowledge, no one complained. But they did encourage me to take lessons. In time, I developed a good ear for music and learned to play adequately. The atmosphere in this church was one of grace and acceptance, a healthy place for children to grow in faith.

The people in our congregation came from several Slavic countries. Services were conducted in Ukrainian but we often invited evangelists from Russia, Poland, Germany, Romania and the United States to speak. We didn't need interpreters because everyone had a basic understanding of all these languages. We sang from English, Ukrainian, Polish and Russian hymn books.

In the mid 1950s, Fred Shelestowsky became our pastor. I loved this man for his tender-hearted, soft-spoken ways. He often wept during his sermons and prayers. I grew up under the leadership of pastors and evangelists who were deeply committed to Jesus and His message. They spoke with enormous passion about their love for Him and His goodness to them. They inspired me to become a true follower of Jesus. Evangelists often stayed for three weeks, preaching every night. Our family seldom missed a service. I listened in awe as they expounded on the scriptures. They also told of harrowing personal life experiences, times when God intervened in miraculous ways to rescue them. My spine tingled as their faith in God's power impacted me. Our church was never dull. Time flew by because every minute was interesting.

My childhood was centered on family and church life. My four best friends came from the congregation. Occasionally, we went to one another's homes on Sunday afternoons. I always enjoyed getting away from my big family for a few hours.

Visiting evangelists usually stayed in our home, though we had less room than other church families. My mother relocated three or four children to give our guests a room to themselves. She prepared their meals and washed their clothes, without complaint. In my opinion, people took advantage of Mom's kind nature. Later, friends pointed out that I allowed others to take advantage of me. Like my mother, if I can make people feel good, it gives me pleasure.

Looking back, it seems impossible that Mom birthed and raised nine children, worked beside my father on the farm every day, cooked endless meals and still managed to run an inn for itinerant speakers.

Later, my father became the pastor of our Slavic church, a position he remained in for more than thirty years, without salary. Dad also took over a publishing company from Toronto that printed gospel tracts and resource material in the Slavic languages. He moved the presses onto his property in Waterford. Dad wrote and published his life story in Ukrainian and distributed it in Eastern Europe. His book sold out and was eventually reprinted without his permission. Dad cares little about copyrights. All that matters to him is that his story is being read, and through it, people are finding Jesus.

My father and I recorded an album of gospel music in Ukrainian and Russian. It too was distributed to the Slavic churches in Canada and to churches in Communist countries. Throughout his life, Dad has built a strong witness for Christ in our community. Local people call him *The Jesus Man*. Our newspaper did an article about Dad and titled it *In God He Trusts*. Dad has never lost his zeal for God nor his love for people.

In my youth, prayer and Bible reading filled our home. As new followers of Jesus, my parents established a godly foundation for our family. I'm a beneficiary of this. My home life and my church life strongly influenced my adult years. The decisions I made later, for my marriage, my children and my career are rooted in the training I received in childhood. Growing up in that little Slavic church where the leaders simply took the Bible and taught us from it gave me a solid spiritual foundation.

I was raised amongst people who suffered tragedies and troubles. They wept when they told how God helped them through their difficulties. Their humility and intense love for the Lord rubbed off on me. By eight or nine years of age, I eagerly anticipated church meetings. In those days, we didn't segregate children from the congregation. We worshiped as one body, old and young. I'm a firm believer that this is a better way to raise godly children. Let them get to know adults, hear their prayers, see them weep with concern and worship with gratefulness. This creates an atmosphere where children are mentored in their faith. They take in much more than we realize. Years later, when I think of these people, I can hear them praying. They stood firm in their faith in spite of hardships. What good role models they were for me.

Our church was made up of several close-knit families with two common bonds: our suffering during World War II and our calling from Jesus to follow Him. Sunday school teachers taught Bible stories in broken English with no manuals or resources, other than the scriptures. They simply asked the Holy Spirit to anoint their words. As children, we had little to distract us in that poor assembly. There, I learned to love Jesus and I have never lost that love. He's been a faithful Friend to me in good times and bad. I consider myself a child of privilege, not in material possessions, but I was born with the silver spoon of a fine Christian heritage.

My father and mother supported our family with long hours of hard work. They exhibited extreme generosity, of their time, their money and their home. They made sure no one they knew went without the necessities of life. They had little but gave much. When visitors left our home, Mom sent them off with farm produce, homemade bread, butter, eggs and baked goods. Of course, she prepared plenty of good Ukrainian food – cabbage rolls and perogies. The aroma of our home is engraved in my memory. No wonder all the evangelists wanted to stay at the Senko's. Money was scarce but everyone ate well.

Chapter 5

Romance and Marriage

The Nunn family lived across the street from our farm. They had a son my age. I couldn't stand Ernie Nunn. My Dad used to tease me and say, "Some day you're going to marry that boy." At age fourteen, I began to notice Ernie's dark-haired good looks. He soon realized he'd caught my attention and wrote several love notes to me. Once, I expressed a craving for potato chips and Ernie walked a mile to the store and returned with a bag of chips for me. With two strong attributes – good looks and romance - Ernie stole my heart.

Soon, the whole neighbourhood recognized Ernie and me as boyfriend and girlfriend. We couldn't date because my eight brothers and sisters tagged along behind us wherever we went. Sometimes we'd drag them to a little restaurant where we'd eat hot dogs but we seldom had a minute alone.

As the oldest of nine, I rarely felt special. Since age four, I'd been my mother's helper and care-taker to my younger siblings. Ernie's attentiveness made me feel beautiful and desirable. His love caused me to see myself as more than a responsible big sister who cooked and cleaned. I often wished Ernie and I could hide from my snoopy brothers and sisters. They created a lot of work for me and every time they saw us kiss they tattled to Mom and Dad. Frustrated, I wanted to bang their heads together. I did whack my sister Patsy's head on the kitchen counter after she snitched to Dad that Ernie had kissed me. I got into trouble for hurting her. At the time, it was worth it.

I yearned for a life free of kids and home responsibilities. That opportunity came when Ernie asked me to marry him. On a glorious day in 1964, at eighteen, I married my sweetheart. Rev. Mike Derkatch, a well-known Slavic pastor from Toronto, performed our wedding ceremony. My dreams of a happily ever-after life with my good-looking, attentive husband got off to a good start. Years of wedded bliss, like rose petals, scented the road ahead of us. At least, that's what I thought.

My mother cried when I left home. Janie, the youngest, was only a year old. Mom didn't know how she'd get along without me. After my marriage to Ernie, I continued to help Mom with the kids. Even after I started working full-time, I spent my days off working in the fields and grading vegetables.

Romance And Marriage

Every Saturday, I cleaned for Mom. My younger sisters helped with farm duties but didn't feel bound to my parents' work or their worries like I did. They socialized with friends and went to the beach, things I hadn't done. One reason my younger siblings didn't move into my position in the family is that Mom didn't think anyone could run her house as well as I did. Even after my marriage, her approval remained an important factor in my life.

I liked my quiet life with Ernie, away from the chaos of our busy farm. We lived near our parents and saw them often but, at the end of a visit, we had our own tidy nest to return to.

In 1965, our first child, Paul, was born. Ernie and I enjoyed parenthood. We were happy and still in love then.

My father was the first person to tell Ernie about Jesus. Dad's message of God's love made Ernie eager to hear more. In his early teens, the pastor of a small non-denominational church took Ernie aside and explained to him why he needed to receive Jesus into His life in a personal way. Ernie knew little about the Bible but his heart was tender and open to whatever plans God had for him.

No one in Ernie's family attended church. This made him shy about showing up on the doorstep of a strange building without a special invitation. He also suffered from the perennial teenage worry - not having the right clothes to wear. Ernie remembers listening to radio sermons and once he bought time on a coin-fed television set to watch the famous evangelist, Oral Roberts. A few times he traveled to revival meetings with friends. After we married, he attended the Slavic church with me, but our Polish, Ukrainian, Russian services went right over the head of this English-speaking boy.

For Ernie's sake, I left the Slavic Church in Waterford and we started attending Simcoe Pentecostal Church. There, Ernie gave his life to Christ and developed a desire to read and understand the Bible. Ernie has always liked to participate in deep discussions on matters of faith.

After four years of married life, Ernie decided to become a pastor. He enrolled at Eastern Pentecostal Bible College in Peterborough, Ontario to train for the ministry. I stayed home with three year-old Paul and worked to support us while Ernie studied. Because the school was a distance away, he lived in residence during the week and traveled home every weekend. I wanted to do everything I could to enable Ernie to fulfill his dream of becoming a minister. I didn't see it as merely Ernie's dream, I saw it as God's plan for his life and, therefore, it became God's plan for my life too.

Ernie thrived in seminary. Sitting in classes taught by people who had a wise grasp of the scriptures stimulated his love of learning. A gifted student with a passion for Christian literature and quality preaching, one of Ernie's favorite college pastimes was sitting around a table debating and discussing Bible-related subjects.

Ernie intended to graduate from the three-year seminary program then pastor a church. This would have happened but Ernie's love of ideas and debate got him into a lot of trouble.

Romance And Marriage

MY FATHER, STANDING BEHIND CONCENTRATION
CAMP FENCE BACK ROW, SECOND ON RIGHT

MY PRECIOUS MOTHER, AS A YOUNG GIRL 15 YEARS OLD.
P.S. THE ONLY PICTURE SALVAGED FROM GERMANY AFTER THE WAR.

MY FATHER WALTER SENKO

SANDRA NUNN AT 8 YEARS OLD

Romance And Marriage

MY FATHER ON THE RIGHT. WALTER SENKO WITH
PASTOR FRED SHELESTOWSKY

THE WATERFORD SLAVIK CONGREGATION STANDING IN FRONT OF
OUR STONE CHURCH WHERE I ATTENDED

ERNIE AND I ON OUR WEDDING DAY, JANUARY 25TH 1964, YOUNG AND INNOCENT

ERNIE WITH PAUL OUR FIRST BORN 1969

CALVARY QUARTET
LEFT TO RIGHT, EARL WATSON, JACK LECOMTE,
SANDRA NUNN, JIM WALKER, DAVID WALKER

MY ELDEST SON PAUL WIFE SONIA,
GRANDCHILDREN FROM LEFT GRACIE, ALLIE, SAMUEL

MY DAUGHTER ANGIE WITH HER HUSBAND BRUCE

OUR GRANDDAUGHTER EMILY NUNN

NOAH NUNN OUR GRANDSON

OUR FIRST GRANDCHILD STEPHEN BONNETT

He Loves Me Not . . .He Loves Me

OUR SON CHRISTOPHER & DAUGHTER-IN-LAW HEATHER.

OUR GRANDCHILDREN, ELIAS, ZEPHANIAH, AZARIA NUNN

ERNIE AND I AS WE ARE NOW. PRAISE GOD.

Chapter 6

The Explosion

*W*hen Ernie's first year of Bible College ended, he returned home to work for the summer months. Following my family's tradition of opening their home to strangers, that summer, Ernie and I offered another student from the college, who had summer employment in the area, living space in our house.

Ernie and this other student engaged in many deep discussions. They sometimes disagreed but always in the spirit of good-natured debate. Their debates remained friendly until one day Ernie's ideas on a certain subject alarmed and angered the other student.

Ernie wrote about this incident in his book, *A Second Chance to Dance*: *Some of my thoughts stepped over the line of acceptability in the student's mind and this person felt obliged to inform a church elder of what they perceived as a daring defiance on my part toward the teachings and practices of some churches in our fellowship.*

The Explosion

Ernie's observations on the subject may have been unusual, I don't know, but he felt safe expressing his opinions on all matters in his own home. He assumed this fellow student was mature enough to consider all aspects of a topic without becoming upset. This was a wrong assumption.

Instead of having an honest face-to-face conversation with Ernie about his views, this student voiced his concerns to one of our church leaders. This leader accepted the student's interpretation of the discussion, and without speaking to Ernie privately, confronted him in front of a large crowd several days later. With no first-hand knowledge of what had actually transpired in the original two-person conversation, people turned against Ernie.

Of this troubling turn of events, Ernie wrote:

"I found it totally incomprehensible how something as insignificant as a simple talk between two students could cause such a stir and demand such urgency. To this day, I have never learned why this became a central issue for my accusers. The entire event left me feeling humiliated and planted a seed of bitterness in my heart and mind."

When Ernie realized his words had been misinterpreted, he approached his accusers and tried to reconcile. They rebuffed his attempts. Their dismissive attitude deeply wounded Ernie. Previous to this incident, he was treated with kindness and respect in our church.

The more he tried to undo the knots of this misunderstanding, the more tangled they became. What began as a minor difference of opinion at our kitchen table erupted into a major church dispute with more people than necessary involved in it. Sadly, the matter didn't end with our church.

Church leaders informed the Bible College of Ernie's *alarming views*. Without warning, Ernie received the most devastating blow of all. A letter arrived from the College denying him the opportunity to return for his second year. Our plans for a career in ministry evaporated so quickly it left us both in shock.

I could see us getting past this setback, but Ernie couldn't. He was shattered.

Ernie could have apologized for his part in the confusion and walked away from it but he became obsessed with the idea that he had been misunderstood. He felt desperate for people to know his side of the story but no one wanted to know his side. Young in years, and in the Christian faith, Ernie descended into extreme distress. He lashed out at the people who caused his pain. Night and day, bitter feelings ate away at him, eventually destroying his personality. Soon, his once tender heart became like rock.

During this whole unnecessary chapter in our lives, one elderly pastor, a man neither of us knew well, put his arm around Ernie and tried to console him. Though his comforting words didn't ease Ernie's pain at the time, this man is still remembered for his godly attitude. He didn't accuse or rebuke, he loved. He was a man, much like my father, who cared more about developing relationships with people than holding to the letter of unwritten laws. Reaching out to a hurting person in love makes all the difference.

Ernie wanted and needed compassion from his friends but he didn't get it.

I won't give all the details about this horrible time in our lives because most of the hurtful things said and done are now forgotten and I don't wish to dredge up old troubles and lay them at the feet of people who have also forgotten them. Long ago, I forgave every person involved in this destructive episode in our lives. I've relinquished all the hurt that resulted from it to Jesus and I want to leave it with Him.

Betrayal and rejection shook Ernie to the core. His self-worth plummeted. He became increasingly angry about the injustice done to him. He changed from an affectionate husband into a mean-spirited, verbally abusive man who became a stranger to me.

In the beginning, I tried to help him work through his feelings by buying helpful books and encouraging him to read them. His response was always, "You think you're better than I am."

My attitude toward this messy incident was different than Ernie's. I saw it as a big fuss that would blow over and soon be forgotten. Ernie couldn't forget. He was crushed.

Every day Ernie seethed against the church and the people who had caused his pain. What began as a trivial disagreement turned into a mountain of misery that affected our marriage and family for decades. As often happens with unresolved conflict, Ernie's sorrow over his losses didn't decrease with time, his sorrow increased. I wanted to help him but I didn't know how. He'd suffered a grave injustice and couldn't let go of it. To add to his grief, he knew I didn't understand and presumed I didn't care.

Our marriage relationship began to fall apart. We lost the love we once had for one another. Over a period of many years, my feelings for Ernie became contemptuous and though we continued to live in the same house, I carved out a life for myself that didn't include my husband. We kept separate bedrooms and separate lives. On several occasions, I asked him to leave. He refused and said it was his house too and he wasn't going anywhere.

Life with Ernie became unbearable. I sought advice from Christian counselors and was advised to leave him. Many times, I came close to walking away from my marriage. Then, I'd remember the vows I made as a young bride, pledging before God to remain with Ernie forever. As impossible as it seemed to keep those vows, I was determined to try.

At times, I'd be encouraged by a glimmer of hope. The old Ernie would reappear. And I would think that all was well again. Then, as fast as it had come, the hopeful glimmer would disappear. I remained in a constant state of indecision – should I leave my husband or continue to live with the angry man he had become.

We seldom went anywhere together. I found it easier to attend church and other functions by myself because Ernie set me on edge.

The Explosion

The massive chip on his shoulder caused him to respond to people and situations with inappropriate anger. His outbursts embarrassed me. Ernie stayed angry for so long, I became detached from him and weary of his rage. I lost respect for him. The caring, sensitive, romantic man I married vanished.

Ernie developed painful headaches, sometimes accompanied by nosebleeds. He found concentration exhausting. For hours he sat in his chair, unable to keep up with daily tasks. An inch at a time, his rage took over our home. It ruled our family, ruined our marriage and destroyed Ernie's relationship with Jesus. Once a fervent Christian, he turned against Christ with as much enthusiasm as he had followed Him. He burned with indignation, against the church as a whole, and believers individually.

After this explosive event, I continued attending the same church. Ernie saw this as a personal betrayal. In his mind, I had sided with his enemies. He saw me as 'one of them.' He wanted me to share his outrage. I didn't agree with the way church leaders handled the situation but I also couldn't support Ernie's irrational response to the offence. Ernie developed a toxic, destructive attitude to spiritual life. I believe when a husband or wife stops making godly choices, the worst thing the other spouse can do is join them in their outrage.

The church was across the street from our home so Ernie easily observed the comings and goings of the congregation. Seeing the people who caused his pain continue on with their lives as if nothing had happened, made forgiveness unthinkable for him. He'd ask, "Why don't they come and visit me?" I couldn't answer that question.

Occasionally, Ernie chose to go to church with me and the children, but on those occasions, he always found something to complain about. He wanted me to join him in his complaints but I refused. The more powerless Ernie felt to control me, and the church, the worse his behavior became.

I had to lead the way and be the example to our children. The body of Christ was, and still is, a lifeline for strength and comfort for me.

Chapter 7

Life in my Dysfunctional Home

Our second child, Angie, was born in 1970 followed by Christopher, in 1973. Even though our relationship was disintegrating, Ernie helped with the children and with household chores and he remained a good provider. As the kids grew, they became aware of their father's rage. They overheard the cruel things Ernie said to me and they hated that. Whenever we argued, the children sided with me. Ernie never harmed me physically; he attacked with verbal darts that shredded my self-confidence and affected me emotionally. He looked for ways to criticize and humiliate me.

Not one to slink away from an argument, I often screamed, "Shut up!" The Nunn home wasn't a pleasant place for our children.

When being in the same house with Ernie became too much for me, I'd pile the kids in the car and take off for a few hours. Short escapes cleared my head. Living with someone who hates you is demoralizing and exhausting. I longed for a peaceful home, but often, for a few hours of peace I had to get away from my husband. When the kids and I returned from these excursions, Ernie acted as if nothing had happened. He erupted with volcanic outbursts, seemingly without cause. But, after an explosion of anger, he calmed, and we experienced temporary peace.

Ernie's thinking became irrational. He constantly mulled over the details of why he hated the church. I'd heard it a thousand times and I didn't want to hear it again. He picked apart the events one by one and analyzed them to death. He had no other audience for his arguments, but me. He was a tormented soul and, in turn, he tormented me.

At work, Ernie had no problems getting along with people but at home he was a different person. When the children became old enough to know that our family life was abnormal, they pleaded for me to leave him. They wanted to escape our unhappy home and live somewhere else, anywhere, free from their father's rage.

If Ernie had committed adultery, I would have left him. But, throughout the years we slept in separate rooms and led separate lives, he remained faithful. Although I often left the house for a few hours to let him cool off, I never left with the intention of staying away, not even for a full day.

Ernie's rages frightened me and the children. Something unexplainable would set him off and he'd take out his fury on the nearest object. Often that meant he destroyed something I cared about. Once, he grabbed our Christmas tree from the living room and heaved it outside. These outbursts never made sense to me.

During one of his peaceful phases, Ernie bought me a Bible. Later, in a rage, he ripped it to shreds. He ranted, spit, swore, smashed holes in walls and broke dishes. His unreasonable and unpredictable behavior caused severe tension in our home.

Ernie's behavior embarrassed me on many occasions. In an attempt to get even with him, one day when he came home and handed me his pay check, I ripped it into little bits. He was upset because he didn't want to explain to his employer why he needed a replacement check. At the time, I didn't care. Tearing up something that mattered to him gave me a measure of revenge for all the times he'd embarrassed me.

Guilt sometimes took hold of Ernie. Whenever this happened, he became remorseful and wanted to get right with God. He refused to attend the church that had hurt him so he would ask, "Why don't you go with me to a different church?"

I refused because I knew he'd find something wrong with every church we attended. He would leave in a huff then I'd be alone in unfamiliar surroundings. I remained with the same church family. People in that congregation understood my situation and prayed for me. They loved and accepted me and my children. We needed the comfort, friendship and stability that come from being part of a Christian community for a long time.

Ernie never gave up the idea that the ones who hurt him needed to ask his forgiveness. He often badgered me to phone certain ones and tell them to come over and say how wrong they'd been to shun him. As years passed, the number of people at the church who remembered the incident dwindled. Phoning anyone to ask for an apology didn't make sense.

In exasperation, I told Ernie to call these people himself, that I wouldn't do it. Finally, he stopped harassing me about making phone calls. For my own wellbeing, I refused to participate in Ernie's rages. He wanted me to be angry at people because he was angry with them. Ernie had a serious problem. Sympathizing with him wouldn't have helped.

I needed to hang onto my sanity. For that reason, I refused to give in to any of Ernie's unreasonable demands. Each time I did this, I gained an important victory, for me, and for my children.

The children attended church with me. Ernie didn't like this but they needed the church as much as I did. I looked forward to a couple of peaceful hours each week in a sanctuary of worship. The services encouraged me, but I grew to anticipate Sundays with fear. While I dressed the kids and myself, Ernie ranted. He especially liked calling me a hypocrite. I longed for harmony in my home, but there was little of it on Sundays.

The car often became a haven for me and the kids. I did a lot of my praying as we drove around. I told them the Bible stories I heard as a child in the Slavic church. As they matured, each of my three children developed a love for books. They read contentedly in the back seat while I drove and prayed.

More than anything, I wanted to pass my Christian heritage on to my children. When they became teenagers, they participated in youth and other church activities and no longer depended on me for spiritual instruction.

Year after year, Ernie slipped farther and farther away from me, our children, and God. Counselors advised me to forsake my hopeless marriage. They said it would be the best decision for me and my children. I can't fully explain why I didn't leave Ernie. Perhaps I'm incurably stubborn. Another part of the answer is that I never completely lost hope for him. I reasoned that the sweet boy across the street, handsome and romantic, couldn't be lost forever. That person must still exist within the personality of my angry husband.

As the years passed, it became almost impossible for me to recall my adoring, young husband.

Living with Ernie became emotionally unsafe. I hid my feelings and thoughts, afraid if I said the wrong thing, he would attack with insults. His hateful words pierced my heart like a knife. I lived behind a wall. My friends and family saw the same fun-loving Sandra I'd always been, but I kept the real me hidden from Ernie. He became a stranger who lived on the other side of my protective wall.

My young bride dreams of a happy-ever-after life with Ernie turned into a nightmare. We dwelt under the same roof but I lived like a widow. I'm sure many people assumed I was a widow because they never saw me with my husband.

I had several close friends who knew about my troubled marriage – one couple and a few women. I was honest with them about happenings in my home. They understood my pain and supported me. They cried with me when I became distraught and encouraged me when I lost hope. Two of them lived to see the change in Ernie and today they share my amazement at God's miracle.

My friends knew how to pray and I needed their prayers. Prayer is a more powerful force than anyone realizes. Often, the Lord lifted me out of deep pits of discouragement because others prayed for me. Without their prayers, patience and kindness, I couldn't have hung on for a miracle.

I don't put on a false face. I let my sorrow show. Some Christians find that kind of honesty difficult. They hide imperfections, afraid other Christians will judge them harshly. Sadly, this happens too often. But, living truthfully makes a person stronger. Honesty helped me cope with a troubled life. An honest talk with a friend, followed by prayer, was often the very thing I needed to lift me out of despair. Besides confiding in friends, I vented in my journals. I let pain flow from my soul onto the pages uninhibited. This practice helped me. I needed to express my feelings. On re-reading my private diaries, I see them as those of a deeply troubled woman.

I wasn't a totally innocent party in our marriage. Some of the ditzy things I did got on Ernie's nerves. I found them funny. But

Life In My Dysfunctional Home

Ernie didn't. Once, depressed and upset, I walked out of the house and left him with the kids. It was a rainy, foggy night, unfit for driving but even low visibility couldn't deter me from heading to Brantford for some retail therapy. On the way home, I wept all over the steering wheel calling on God to deliver me from all my troubles. I heard a bump under the car but paid no attention. A voice yelled, "What are you doing?" Two men appeared through the fog waving at me to stop. I looked around and realized I had somehow turned onto the railroad tracks. Embarrassed, I kept going, thinking I would come to a place where I could turn off the tracks and get back onto the road. But the car's wheels got stuck on the rails. I couldn't move backward or forward. The two men ran to my rescue, jacked the car up and somehow these good Samaritans put this crazy woman back on the road to home. While they worked on my car, I looked ahead and realized if I'd kept going, I would've driven into the river. This mishap wrecked the whole undercarriage of the car. In typical fashion, I thought the whole episode funny and laughed about it with my friends. To Ernie, and I'm sure most other husbands, it wasn't a bit funny.

Another time when I needed to get away from the house, I went to a fast-food drive-through and ordered a baked potato, my way of drowning my sorrows. "Without sour cream," I said. When the server handed it to me, I took a huge bite and sour cream exploded all over me. In a panic, I opened the car door and jumped out, forgetting to put the car in park. I stood, mouth open, baked potato in hand, clothes covered in sour cream and watched my car roll into a picnic table. A crowd gathered to stare. Everyone breathed a sigh of relief when the driverless vehicle stopped at the river's edge. Again, I'd come close to sinking my car in the river. When the car stopped, I ran, jumped in and backed it up. Weirdly, I was more upset about the sour cream than the table-size gouge in my car's front end. I circled through the drive-through to let the server know he'd caused a lot of damage by flubbing my order.

I pitched the potato in the garbage and started for home, worried about how I would explain the dents to Ernie. I drove to my son's house first and asked him what I should tell his father. "Just say you hit a picnic table," he said. How simple. I would've gone into a lengthy explanation about how the server mixed up my order, how I jumped out of the car, how the crowd of on-lookers gasped, how funny the car looked traveling without a driver, on and on. Again, I saw the humorous side of this incident. Ernie didn't. He put up with a lot of silliness from me.

My family loved Ernie in spite of his cruelty to me. In return, he treated them with respect. Every Saturday, he helped me clean my parents' house and often worked in the fields beside them. They knew about his mean side but they chose to see goodness in him. My parents didn't interfere in our troubled relationship. They didn't criticize Ernie or advise me to leave him. I sometimes vented about my husband but I didn't want Mom and Dad, or any of my friends, to criticize him. Perhaps that's pride. I'm not sure. It's just how I felt.

In the same way a child needs a parent, Ernie needed me. He wouldn't have fared well alone. I knew that even if he didn't acknowledge it. Being needed was a familiar feeling for me. For that reason, staying in a loveless marriage may have been easier for me than for other wives.

Chapter 8

My Search for Significance

A steady torrent of Ernie's cruel comments damaged my self-esteem. Affirmation from other sources became important to me. I'd come a long way since learning to play piano with one finger. My parents had enrolled me in lessons and I developed a good ear for music.

When four men from our church formed *The Calvary Quartet*, they recruited me to accompany them. Invitations to sing flowed in from churches all over Ontario. At certain times of the year, we spent every weekend on the road. As a social person, I enjoyed traveling with the gang and meeting new people who admired and appreciated me.

Sometimes Ernie complained about my absences, and a few times he forbade me to go with the quartet, but in the end, he usually relented and agreed to watch the children. One of the singer's wives traveled with us and became my best friend. It was a cozy arrangement and one that helped me survive a terrible home life. No matter how bad things got, I walked into a different world on the weekends. Grateful audiences helped to fill my need for significance.

Being part of a popular musical group had a dark side – I experienced a lot of guilt about leaving my children with their father. I was glad to escape Ernie for a few hours, but at same time, I felt guilty about leaving him to watch the kids after he'd worked all week. A nagging conscience didn't stop me though. My association with the quartet lasted fifteen years. The sense of freedom and enjoyment I received became more important to me than it should have. Years later, I apologized to Ernie for abandoning him and the children on so many weekends.

Besides playing for the quartet, I participated in many church activities. As in childhood, I found my identity there. The church provided my children and me with a life outside our war-torn home.

Since childhood, I've sought to make my mark. When an idea comes to mind, I go for it. This straight-ahead approach to life keeps me busy. After accepting the position of Cook at our church's day-care center, I enrolled in a two-year course at Mohawk College in Hamilton. Graduation from this course fully qualified me for the job. At the time, three of our grandchildren lived with us. I also cleaned weekly for my mother and, in spite of the animosity between us, Ernie and I worked side by side in our housecleaning business.

Chapter 9

Queen of Clean and Clutter Control

*A*s the relationship with my husband deteriorated, I sought attention in other places. For several years my obsession with order and cleanliness gave me a platform that more than filled my need for significance.

I know how to run a clean and orderly home. Organization comes easy to me. It's like breathing. Everything in my home is clean, not only on the surface, but behind the scenes - inside cupboards, closets and ovens, all the hidden places.

My passion for cleanliness began when we lived on the farm. At an early age, my mother taught me to clean under beds and to wash baseboards, walls and trim. Crumbs and dirt attract mice, bugs and germs she said. Every surface must be clean.

Co-workers from our church's day-care center, where I've worked for over twenty-five years, often drop in for coffee after hours. My home, across the street, is convenient for them. On these visits, they often asked how I managed to keep my home organized and clean while working full-time and raising three grandchildren. Their question gave me an idea.

Living in a clean house is a satisfying experience for me but I never intended to make a business out of it until the 1990s. That's when I marketed my obsession for cleanliness. I approached TV Ontario with my ideas to conquer clutter and maintain a clean home. TVO came to my house with cameras for a full day of shooting. They opened closets and cupboards and asked me to walk viewers through the steps of keeping an orderly home.

There's no magic to cleanliness and clutter control. I advise people to purge their closets and to put things where they're most likely to look for them, whatever place seems practical. After the TVO documentary, people started asking for my help in organizing their homes. I developed a clientele of people who sought my advice.

In my home visits, I see the worst of it. Houses that haven't been properly cleaned in years, cobwebs hanging from ceilings and storage boxes piled in corners. By the end of some visits, my head aches and I wonder what critters might be nesting amongst all the dirt, dust and stuff.

I approached Fanshawe College about teaching a program called *The Working Person and Total Home Organization*. These classes became popular and led to other workshops and seminars. The local school board hired me to teach staff at a Professional Development Day. At first, these sessions intimidated me but I soon lost my nervousness, because when it comes to cleanliness and organization, I know what I'm talking about.

At my seminars, I tell people, "Don't defend your clutter. If you do, there's no helping you." People come up with endless excuses for dirt and disorder. It's either the children's fault, or the husband's fault. Even children as young as two can pick up their toys. My students like it when I tell them the sexiest thing alive is a man pushing a vacuum cleaner.

My classes rock with laughter. When I describe a cluttered home, people snicker with embarrassment and often say, "She's talking about me."

Students started inviting me to their homes for personal consultations. Some homes overflow with stuff. It's hard to walk from one end to the other without tripping. "Stuff," I tell them, "is a dirty word. You have to rid your life of dirt. That means getting rid of stuff."

I became known as the *Queen of Clean and Clutter Control*. The Toronto Star wrote a two-page article about me and titled it, *Queen of Clean on a Clutter Crusade*. Local and national newspaper articles followed. People liked what they saw on the TVO documentary and wanted to know more. A mid-day television program out of Toronto, asked me to stay in the city and tape segments for their show. I don't have a natural love of the podium, but when it comes to keeping house, I can talk all day.

My classes and seminars generated more clients. As much as I love cleaning, I also love meeting and chatting with people. This new career gave me a chance to talk about my biggest passion, outside of the Lord Jesus, and it also brought many new friends into my life.

I compiled a simple manual on how to organize and clean a home. These booklets sell by the dozens at speaking engagements and workshops. Students often say that I should have my own television program - a combination home organization and comedy show. I don't try to be funny but when I'm relaxed and in my comfort zone, my natural humour flows.

Cleaning and clutter control became my evening career. In the daytime, I continued to work at our church's daycare center.

With an unbearable home life, I sought validation elsewhere and found it by teaching what I know best – cleaning and de-cluttering. At home, I remained a nobody, my personality smothered by Ernie's insults and unpredictable tantrums. As pianist for the quartet, and later, as Queen of Clean and Clutter Control, I found significance.

I also learned to step up to a microphone with confidence. This experience prepared me for the ministry Ernie and I have today - telling the story of how God saved our marriage.

I still get invited into homes to give advice and occasionally I do seminars on cleanliness and organization, but my priority, since 2003, is telling people about the miracle the Lord did in my marriage.

Chapter 10

Adjusting to my new Husband

*A*fter Christmas Day 2003 my life changed. Ernie's God-encounter shook up our household. It wasn't easy for the children, or me, to accept the change in him. We wanted to but it took time for us to realize his was a permanent and total transformation. With kindness and patience, Ernie proved himself to us. Instead of wild outbursts of anger, he exhibited tolerance and gentleness. It was almost too much for us to comprehend. But, we had to acknowledge that something amazing had happened to him. The misunderstanding in the church had sent Ernie into a dark place. This new experience filled him with peace.

After my initial skepticism, I couldn't help but respond to Ernie's love. In times past, Ernie had occasionally expressed a desire to change, but his strength came from mere human effort, not from God. He couldn't keep up his good intentions and quickly slid back into rage and abuse. As a child, I'd seen God work many miracles. I believed in His power and willingness to heal the sick and fix impossible situations. After the events of Christmas 2003, I began to recognize His fingerprint on Ernie's life – the tender heart, easy tears, and a willingness to ask others to forgive him – these are telltale signs that God is at work.

We'd been sleeping in separate rooms for years. I had my room just the way I liked it – spotless and perfect, my sanctuary. I didn't want men's underwear and socks on my floor. Part of me wanted our estrangement to continue. I had learned to cope with the old Ernie. Change, even good change, sometimes requires difficult adjustments.

God had given Ernie and me a second chance at love and that meant I had to open the doors of my sanctuary and invite my husband to come in. When I did that, an amazing outpouring of affection came into our relationship. We became like a young married couple again. Our grandchildren, who live with us, noticed a big difference in Ernie and in the way we treated each other. They said, "Look, Papa and Gramma are in the same bed." They'd never seen that before. To them, it was astonishing.

Our new love filled me with excitement. I told co-workers and neighbours, and anyone who would listen, what God had done for my hopeless marriage. "My husband loves me," I said. "Can you believe it? He really loves me."

I don't consider myself a desirable woman, not the kind of woman men become infatuated with. What my husband shows me is genuine love, not passing fascination.

Three months after we started sharing the same room, Ernie had a heart attack. I don't know if it resulted from our new found joy of sex, but clearly, the excitement was more than Ernie's heart could bear. His attack wasn't a serious one and he recovered quickly. Later, in 2008, he had a more serious attack that required two weeks in hospital.

One night, after we went for dinner, Ernie kissed me outside the restaurant. I said, "People will think we're having an affair because old married couples like us don't kiss in public."

Ernie replied, "Yes, I am having an affair, an affair with my wife."

The romantic boy I knew as a teenager came back to me. Ernie isn't shy about public displays of affection. He tells everyone how much he loves me. He often says, "I've found something sweeter than sugar, my wife."

Recently, Ernie and I sat on our son's front porch, rocking gently on a swing built for two. Two acres of beautiful flower gardens stretched out before us, an amazing sight. I said, "Isn't this nice? We're sitting here, our bodies touching."

Ernie said, "We have to be together now more than ever."

At one time, we would have crowded to the far edges of that swing and not allowed our bodies to touch. At that moment, I thought that I never want to be without Ernie. We talk a lot. And

Adjusting To My New Husband

pray together. But, we also sit in comfortable silence. This is a sign of a healthy relationship.

Ernie is a true servant. That part of his character showed in him as a young man but anger and resentment ruined the best parts of his personality. His true personality has returned. He looks for ways to make me feel beautiful. He runs to open car doors, tucks me gently into the car seat. He says he's making up for all the times he slammed doors in my face and treated me with disdain.

Our marriage went through a total transformation. My sons built new friendships with their Dad. Now, they're closer to him than to me. They ask his advice and seek his involvement in their lives. It gives me pleasure to see this after decades of estrangement between my children and Ernie. My daughter, and our grandchildren, also embraced their new father and grandfather.

After our miracle, I told everyone – "My husband who once despised me now loves me and I love him."

Many women came to see how my crazy home had changed. I told the girls at work. I told the servers at the coffee shop. I told total strangers. And everyone I told wanted to hear more. People need to hear what Jesus can do in a home.

In the horrible days, I told young people they were out of their minds to get married. I really believed that. I knew good marriages existed but disappointment with mine and the pain of having my husband turn against me tainted my impression of marriage.

Today, Ernie and I look forward to growing old together.

Chapter 11

Crossing the Street

At the time of our miracle, I was still attending the same church, the one across the street from our home, the one where all the trouble started for Ernie. Thirty-seven years had passed since the explosive event that ruined our marriage. During that time, Ernie rarely attended church with me, and when he did, he always found something wrong with the sermon, the singing or another part of the service. I'd have to listen to his complaints on the way home and for days afterward. I never wanted a replay of those episodes.

The Sunday following that eventful Christmas of 2003, Ernie said, "I want to go to church with you."

I made a disgusted sound. What if someone who remembered the original dispute sidled up to Ernie and reminded him of it? What if he didn't like the pastor? All our trouble started in church and I wasn't able to let go of my fears of a reoccurrence right away.

"You're welcome to go by yourself," I told him. "I've been going by myself for thirty-seven years and I plan to stay home today."

Ernie went to church alone.

In August 2003, before Ernie revealed his God conversation to me, someone at the church had asked him to help with a barbecue. He did. That small occurrence opened the door for Ernie to return. Ernie didn't express his fears about crossing the street but it must have taken courage for him to open the doors and step inside after years of absence. The building didn't fall down. People welcomed and accepted him immediately. Those who knew about Ernie's years of anger were especially thrilled to see him.

After the holiday season ended, at the first opportunity, I rushed into the pastor's office and blurted out, "You won't believe what has happened." Rev. David Kingston didn't know us well and hadn't heard about our marriage. He listened, somewhat flabbergasted, as I told him our entire story. That's the way I do things – full-speed ahead. I didn't realize until I finished that Pastor Kingston had barely uttered a word.

Going back to church was a culture shock for Ernie. He expected to deal with the same type of condemnation he had to deal with in his youth. He prepared himself for that. But he found a more loving and accepting congregation. Soon after returning to the church, Pastor Kingston invited Ernie to sing, which pleased Ernie immensely.

Ernie went to church alone that first Sunday following Christmas. The next Sunday, I went with him. I'd been sitting in the pew by myself for a long time. Ernie held my hand and put his arm around me. It felt unbelievably good to sing and worship God with my husband again. Sunday after Sunday, when we're not on the road fulfilling speaking engagements, we attend our home church together.

After a while, the congregation began to acknowledge the miracle of our renewed marriage. They invited us to tell our story. This became our first speaking engagement. I'm glad our story of a healed relationship was first told in this church. It shows how thoroughly God mends broken hearts and how he turns all things together for good, in His time. I wanted the people in our congregation to be the first ones to know of our miracle. Most of them knew about our fractured relationship because I'm the type of person who tells people everything. It was fitting then that these same people should hear about our miracle.

After telling our story to our home congregation, other churches and organizations invited us to tell it to them.

Chapter 12

Our Mission

Ernie hadn't become an ordained minister as once planned. But, he still had an aptitude for public speaking. Always an excellent student, Ernie studied at home and earned a Bachelor's of Theology degree. During my years as the Queen of Clean and Clutter Control, I became comfortable behind a microphone.

We sent letters to churches, making ourselves available to speak about marriage relationships, mainly by telling our personal story. A few invitations resulted from these letters but most of our engagements have resulted from word of mouth. One person hears our story, relates it to another, then, we receive an invitation. Wherever we share our story, people accept us warmly.

When people see a marriage as terrible as ours transform into something beautiful and full of love, it inspires them to pray that God will work a miracle in their relationships too. It makes them want to persevere instead of taking the easy route of dissolving the marriage.

People tell me I'm transparent, and that's true. It comes naturally to me. I think it's a good thing. I was always truthful about our dysfunctional marriage; now, I'm free to tell how things have changed.

Ernie started singing at our speaking engagements and that part of our ministry took off immediately. More than two thousand copies of his CDs have sold. Gazing at the faces of our listeners from a podium showed me something I hadn't realized. Many Christian marriages are in trouble. I see it on the faces of our listeners when we speak and I hear it from those who linger after meetings to talk personally with us.

Many marriages appear happy, but few are what they seem. Within the Christian community, relationships are falling apart. People paste smiles on their faces but inside they're dying, crying for help. They won't tell anybody because they feel obligated to keep up a 'Christian image.' They don't want to let the church down, or let God down. It's a strange phenomenon that Christians espouse this brand of dishonesty. I don't think we need to tell everyone about our marriage troubles but being honest is the first step to a better marriage – honesty with God first, then with people.

People approach us after meetings to share their relationship sorrows. This is a constant reminder to us that Satan is attacking families and marriages, the foundation of our society. Weakened marriages lead to weakened churches and suffering children, dissension instead of peace. Christ is the only answer.

A few months after we started speaking, Pastor Bruce Martin flew us out to speak to his large congregation in Winnipeg. It was like a honeymoon for us. We spent three wonderful days with Pastor Martin. Years earlier, he had been our pastor in Simcoe. He knew all about the nutty Nunn household.

Rev. Martin made pastoral visits to our house in spite of Ernie's hostility toward the church. Ernie was usually cordial to him but on one occasion he vented his anger. Instead of walking out the door, Pastor Martin responded by telling Ernie that he loved him. Ernie didn't expect that response. His rage instantly evaporated and he walked out of the room like a whipped puppy.

When he was our pastor, Rev. Martin showed up for all our family's celebrations. He picked cucumbers in my parents' field, spent time with my Dad in pastor-to-pastor talk. He is much like Dad in that he cherishes relationships and sincerely cares about people as individuals. Pastor Martin respected Dad as a former pastor and as a man of God. Often in old-age, pastors are shelved, their years of service forgotten and discounted.

Pastor Martin was only in his twenties when he lived in Simcoe but he possessed the wisdom of a seasoned leader. When we told him about our miracle, he cried.

Before we spoke at the Sunday morning service at the Winnipeg Church, Pastor Martin told us to feel free to invite people to come to the altar for prayer when we finished. Three hundred people gathered round the front of that huge sanctuary. One man in his eighties walked up with a handkerchief covering his face. After speaking with him, I knew he did this out of shame. He said with tears, "My wife and I have been mean to each other for decades. Do you think God can help us?" His wife stood beside him, also weeping. I prayed with them and before they returned to their seats, I admonished them to stop destroying one another with cruel words.

Unaccustomed to public ministry, we found speaking difficult, at first. We reminded ourselves that God uses simple people. And we discovered that everyone responds to love. We care. Our audiences sense that when we speak. Love caused Ernie to respond to God. In turn, I responded to Ernie's love for me. Love softens hearts.

It's humbling to see the Holy Spirit move deeply in people when we tell them what God has done for us. We simply tell our story. It's our story that gives people hope. We don't have answers to the complicated problems people share with us but we know Someone who does and that Person isn't reluctant to show His power.

At times, listening to other people's problems weighs heavily on us, but the Bible tells us that by bearing each other's burdens we are fulfilling the law of God. The law of God is love. (Galatians 6:2)

People ask if I regret all those wasted years and if I wish Ernie could have changed sooner. I don't dwell on the past. I simply say, *Lord use us now.* We feel unworthy of our marvelous miracle. We don't understand why the Lord chooses to use us. But since He does, we plan to stand tall and keep telling our story.

Whenever we speak, Ernie sings, then, he tells his side of the story. Afterwards, I tell my side. We're not on the platform for our good looks. And we're not the most talented speakers. I'd like to be more sophisticated, perhaps put on a few airs. But, I can't. People relate to me because I'm honest about what I've been through. It's not uncommon for people to cry as they listen to our story. I see so many tears.

When we first started speaking, I battled with a condemning voice that whispered to me, "Who do you think you are to get up in front of people and speak about marriage?"

This usually happened after I spoke, at night, as I lay awake. This bothered me because I already felt unworthy of being in a position of spiritual leadership. We have an enemy who doesn't want anyone to hear about a loving God. I recognized these negative messages as coming from Satan. Satan continually tries to silence God's followers.

As a child, I learned from the Bible how to handle spiritual battles like this – *"Submit yourselves to God. Resist the devil and he will flee from you." (James 4:7)*

Each time I experience disturbing thoughts of unworthiness, I recommit my life to Jesus and I continue to tell my story. As I keep speaking straight from my heart, the negative whispers diminish.

Perhaps they'll never completely vanish but the Lord is using them to teach me more about spiritual warfare.

I've also battled the enemy on another issue. Every once in a while, fear stirs inside me. I wonder: *Is my miracle too good to be true? Could it fall apart?* When fear intimidates me with thoughts like this, I rebuke them in the name of Jesus. Satan is the author of fear. God fills me with peace. Satan wants to plant doubt in my mind, but I won't allow it because my life belongs to the Lord Jesus.

"For God has not given us the spirit of fear; but of power, and of love, and of a sound mind." 2 Timothy 1:7.

When we first started speaking together at meetings, when my turn came, I would go to the microphone and begin by saying, *"I'm not really a speaker but..."*

A few people approached me and said they liked the way I told my story but that I shouldn't begin by saying I wasn't a speaker. It drew attention to me, they said, and away from our story. I stopped saying those words. My duty before God is to tell what He has done for us. Whether I'm a gifted speaker, or not, doesn't matter. I want people to focus on the love story God is writing in our lives, not on my inadequacies.

At one church we visited, the pastor shared his heartbreak with us. Several couples in his congregation were on the verge of divorce. He knew of on-going affairs between members. He said, "Tell your story freely. These people need to hear it."

When we finished speaking, we invited people to come to the front of the church for prayer and to re-dedicate themselves to the Lord and to His plan for their marriages. Nearly the whole congregation left their places in the pews and walked to the front of the church. That sight overwhelmed us and confirmed to us that the need for our message is great.

Two Canadian Christian television programs interviewed us: *It's a New Day* and *100 Huntley Street*. After we appeared on these shows, we received many emails, mainly from viewers in their forties, fifties and sixties, people who had been married many years. They wrote us sad and hopeless accounts of marriages on the brink of collapse. That is another reason we need to keep telling our story.

Our listeners often comment that Ernie's love for me shows in his actions. He kisses me, holds my hand and caresses my face. People observe that he runs ahead to open doors. I once wrote in my diary that my husband was a jerk – this was the word I thought best suited him. This same man I once called a jerk is now transformed to the point that even his gestures are a testimony to the miracle God has performed in his life.

When Ernie finishes speaking and introduces me, he does it by telling a story about two farmers. One asks, "Are you a Christian?" The other replies, "Ask my wife." Then I step forward and tell my side of our love story which confirms the truth of what my husband has told the audience. When I tell how Jesus changed Ernie's behavior, our listeners don't doubt Ernie's account of how God awakened him in the night and began a deep transformation in his soul.

My days are long and busy. Without Jesus, I wouldn't have enough stamina to stand up and speak on weekends. My strength comes from Him. Paul wrote these words two thousand years ago and today, I live by them:

"My grace is sufficient for you, for my power is made perfect in weakness. Therefore I will boast all the more gladly about my weaknesses, so that Christ's power may rest on me."(2 Corinthians 12:9)

My whole life I've told everyone about Jesus. This remains my life's goal – to tell as many people as possible about the amazing things God has done for me and especially to tell about my marriage miracle.

Chapter 13

Changes

We called our mother Mama. Some called her Martusha. She and I worked as one, in the house, and in the fields. Beside her, I learned the value of diligence and hard work. My brother, Walter, once told Mama she was a workaholic. The incident became amusing because Mama had never heard of a workaholic. To her work was a good word, with no negative connotations. She thought he called her an alcoholic and was justifiably upset.

It's true that Mama held physical labour in high regard, but she also treasured personal relationships. She toiled in the fields with our hired men. At noon each day, she returned to the house to make lunch for everyone. The workers relaxed and ate but her work continued in the kitchen. After making lunch, serving it and cleaning up, she returned to the fields. As pastor of the Slavic church, my father's attention was often drawn away from the farm to ministering duties. Mama became the mainstay of the farm. She had a well-developed gift for organizing the growing of crops and also for taking her produce to market.

Mama loved her greenhouses and spent hours out there alone. I think the isolation of farming pleased her. A busy family life left little time for reflection and she was a person who valued her quiet moments. At the end of each day, she retreated to the room she shared with my father and sat on the side of the bed. She'd often have her Bible on her knee or on her tummy if she was pregnant. Her lips moved quietly as she prayed. She displayed an attitude of worship and meditation consistently throughout her life. She had a rich relationship with her Savior, Jesus. I often picture her, sitting on the edge of her bed, shutting the world out and letting our Lord in.

After coming to Canada, Mama learned that, soon after her abduction and transfer to Germany, her mother in the Ukraine died, in her early forties. It pained her that she never saw her mother again after age twelve. In the sixties, my parents saved enough money to return to their home country and visit remaining family members. One of Mama's brothers immigrated to Canada and lived with us for a while. She continually wrote letters to family in the old country and sent them money. She also bought clothing and shipped it to them. Often, they sold the things Mama sent and used the money to buy needed farm animals.

In 1987, my brother Walter, at age twenty-nine, died in a car accident about a mile from the Senko farm. He was unmarried and still living at home at the time of his death. Mama took his loss very hard. She understood, better than most, that life brings sorrows as well as joys but this understanding didn't assuage her grief over the death of one of her nine children. She wept from the deepest part of her soul.

On the day Walter died, I went to my parents' home to grieve with them. In a strange way, it comforted me to wash his clothing and clean his room. I'd rocked him as a baby, changed his diapers and dressed him for school. I had co-mothered him. The sadness of his loss broke my heart. Mama and I shared this profound grief. A quiet woman, she didn't express her loss in words; she expressed it in tears.

My mother's heart became enlarged from a lifetime of intense physical exertion. Her health began to deteriorate. Pounds fell off her body. Her strength waned. She weakened to the point of spending many days at a time in bed. After an episode of being bedridden, she would bounce back to good health. This up-and-down phase lasted for a few years.

By 2004, it became apparent that Mama and Dad would have to give up farming. They bought a two bedroom house in Waterford. The transition from a farm to town living meant a major downsize. Because of Mama's health, my sisters and I sorted through her household things, keeping only the best and only what was needed for a smaller home. She had shelves of sheets and mismatched bedding left over from the days when her home had rocked with activity. When she realized we'd purged her things, she sobbed like a child.

It deeply saddened her that she couldn't take all her belongings to the new home.

Mama also mourned the loss of the farm. The fields had been her domain. She loved looking out over the crops, seeing the fruit of her labour. When she was taken from her family, farming became Mama's way of life, first in Germany, then in Canada, where she and my father earned enough money to buy a farm of their own. Farming had been her life's career.

After the move, Mama's health continued to deteriorate. Her role as caregiver completely ended. She became the one who needed care. The hundreds of guests who passed through her home in healthier days were replaced by a few home care workers. She seldom left the house except for medical appointments. Her surroundings included an oxygen tank and a walker. For two years, I went to her place after work each day, and fed her like a child. When I looked at her, it seemed impossible that my once strong and vital mother had become an invalid.

I still picture Mama sitting on the side of her bed counting the money in her wallet after market day. She wasn't a greedy person but it gave her pleasure that her work days resulted in a good pay day. My mother was an intelligent and capable woman but there was an innocence about her that made her seem naïve.

Mama lived to see the change in my marriage to Ernie. For that, I give thanks to God. Our new love pleased her. In her last months, Ernie sat with her and sang her favorite hymns. She told him she loved him. As people often do when they're releasing connections to the earth, she wept a lot.

On April 15, 2006, down to 118 pounds, Mama left this world for the place our Lord Jesus has prepared for everyone who follows Him. I did the eulogy at her funeral. Every time I clean my house, I think of my mother. I miss her daily phone calls, her cooking, especially the Ukrainian dishes, but most of all, I miss her prayers. My siblings and I began, early in life, to depend on our parents' prayers. We learned to pray too, of course, but they seemed to have a direct line to Heaven.

My Father, Walter, still lives in Waterford, Ontario. His health is failing but his mind is filled with thankfulness to His Savior. My parents lived a grateful life. Early hardships caused them to appreciate every good thing that came their way. My brother, Jerry, became a farmer and operates a sandblasting business. Patricia is also a farmer, now retired. Lilly became a school teacher, David pastors a church in Windsor, Ontario and Steven runs a home improvement business in Cleveland, Ohio. Ronnie lives with Dad and is his primary caregiver. Janie is a school principal. We are all grateful for the faith in God my parents passed on to us.

When Ernie and I started speaking, if our engagements were within driving distance, my father came to hear us. He faithfully supported us with his presence until ill health prevented it. We spoke at a few Ukrainian churches. On these occasions, after we finished, Dad would take the microphone and speak to the congregation in

Ukrainian. He gave thanks to God for the miracle in our marriage. Ukrainian and Russian women always sob when we tell our story to them.

My father and I have traveled a long way since our initial meeting at the orphanage and our train trip across Germany to re-unite with Mama. In babyhood, my heart became one with his. And it remains so today.

Chapter 14

My Continuing Love Story

That Christmas in 2003, when I overheard my husband say that he wished he could love his wife as she should be loved, a sense of elation started to grow in my soul. That elation continues to grow.

God did something for me that no psychiatrist or counselor could do. He restored my marriage. He restored Ernie's mind and filled him with peace. Ernie gave up all grudges and holds no malice toward anyone.

My husband, whom I once despised, has become desirable to me. I fell completely in love with him again. And he with me. Our feelings changed from contempt to not being able to get enough of each other. Today, nine years later, we still feel the same.

Ernie and I talk over all our decisions. We don't always agree. It would be abnormal if we did. We handle our disagreements with love and respect. We have more to discuss than most couples our age because we're still raising children. We aren't the first grandparents who have had to step up and provide a home for their grandchildren. And we won't be the last. For as long as I can remember, I've been caring for children. Even my full-time job as a cook is at a daycare center. I wouldn't have chosen these responsibilities for myself but they've come to me in God's providence. I rely on Jesus every day for the strength needed to fulfill His purpose for my life – in my marriage, my home, my ministry and my job.

I'm now the age where most women have retired but I still work full-time. By the time I get home from work, my energy is depleted. My beloved Ernie vacuums, washes dishes, and drives our grandchildren to and from school. He does everything he can to make my life easier.

In the evenings, we take time for ourselves, discuss what's on our minds and pray together. We share lots of kisses and hugs and remember to say 'I love you' often. Ernie calls me at work sometimes just to tell me he loves me. Our family, our neighbours and everyone who knew us before our miracle see how we've changed.

Our three children survived a difficult home life. Today, Paul is a doctor, Angie a nurse and Christopher, a lawyer. (We needed a psychiatrist in our family but we didn't get one.) The children have all forgiven their father. One day, our daughter Angie, called Ernie on the phone and said, "Dad, I love you." It took a lot of courage and forgiveness for her to put her feelings into words. This was the first time she said those words to her dad. Our kids remain in awe of the changes in their father. When they see Ernie and me, the way we are now, so in love again, it makes them forget about all those angry years.

I've never traveled or taken vacations. Work is what I've always known and I'm comfortable with that. When I think of flying to a sunny location just to relax on a beach, I can't picture myself doing it.

God has given us the miracle of a second chance to dance. And He wants to do the same for other couples. At one of our speaking engagements, an elderly woman approached me. I believe she had been married about fifty years. She said, "My husband and I no longer love each other, in fact, we can't stand one another. We've gone for counseling but nothing has worked for us. Will you pray that God will work a miracle in our lives?"

Ernie and I prayed for this woman and her husband. She contacted us later to say that they are experiencing a great improvement in their relationship. Nothing else changes hearts like prayer.

When people listen to our story, they often want us to pray that they will experience the same miracle that we have experienced. It's important to realize that each of us has a different need. No two marriages are exactly the same. God sees into the depths of a person's soul, a place we can't see, and He knows each person's unique need.

It's important to acknowledge that during those dark years, when Ernie was consumed with anger and rage, I had little hope for us. I thought that horrible chapter in our marriage would never end. I suffered through many bouts of loneliness and despondency. Through that prolonged and troubled time, God was with me. I love the song that says, *"He was there all the time,"* because that's the way it was for me. I depended on the Lord every day. If I hadn't, I'd have given in to total despair.

When Ernie and I appeared on 100 Huntley Street, Moira Brown, introduced us as a couple married for forty-four years but happily for only four years. After hearing our story, she asked me a question I often hear: "Why did you stay with Ernie?"

The answer is simple. I loved Ernie, or at least I loved the person he was when I married him. I meant the vow I made to him before the Lord on our wedding day. That vow was for better or worse, not for good times only. Often in life, things don't turn out as expected. My marriage definitely turned out for the worse. Therefore, I placed my trust, not in my marriage, but in the Savior I've loved since childhood. I always knew if anything good came of our marriage, it would be because of God. He is the only One who can take a hateful relationship like ours and make it loving.

After hearing me speak, one woman told me that her husband wasn't as passionate as mine. She asked what she could do to change that. It's important to consider that people show their love in different ways. Some husbands aren't given to open shows of affection but they are loyal, kind and good providers. These attributes shouldn't be downgraded. A man who tosses rose petals in his sweetheart's path may not be any more loving than the one who is less demonstrative. Wives should show appreciation for all the good things their husbands do. As I told my college class, the sexiest thing alive is a man pushing a vacuum cleaner.

Our plan for the future is to keep on telling our love story. If we end up in a senior's residence in our old age, even there, we'll keep sharing it. Ernie is recording a third CD, a Christmas album. On this one, our granddaughter, Emily, sings with him. I am writing another manual on cleanliness and clutter control. This time, I'm writing specifically for seniors.

We've been married now for 48 years but I feel like a new bride. Only a few of these have been happy years but the happy ones have erased the memory of the others. My prayer is that love would be rekindled in marriage relationships and that kindness would reign in families.

When couples live in love and harmony, God is pleased.

A final word from Sandra

*G*od is your anchor. No matter what happens, hold onto Him. He gave me strength to cope with a miserable marriage, and many other difficulties. He'll do the same for you. I weep when I think about His faithfulness to me. I'll never get over the enormity of His kindness. He's still teaching me how to live. I have many things yet to learn.

Love, Sandra

ernestsandranunn@yahoo.ca

Lord, I pray that every person who reads my story will come to know you as The Faithful Friend.

CPSIA information can be obtained at www.ICGtesting.com
Printed in the USA
LVOW130119081112

306332LV00002B/1/P